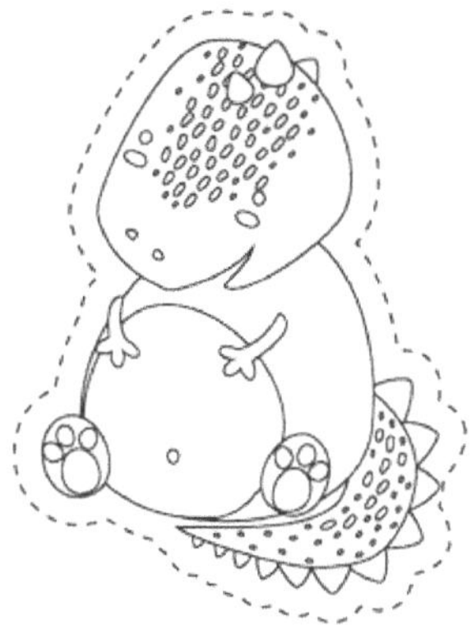

This book belongs to

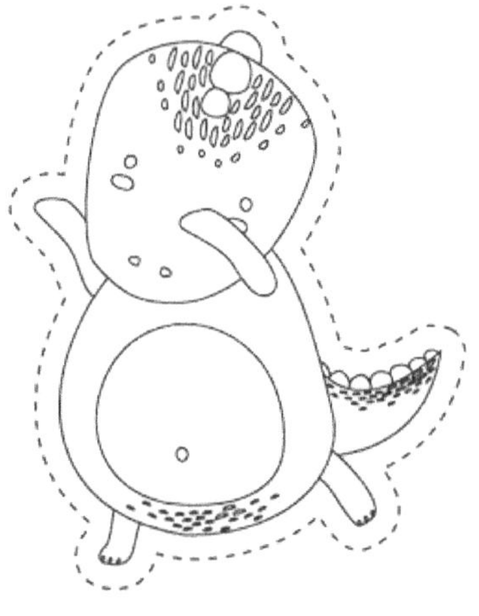

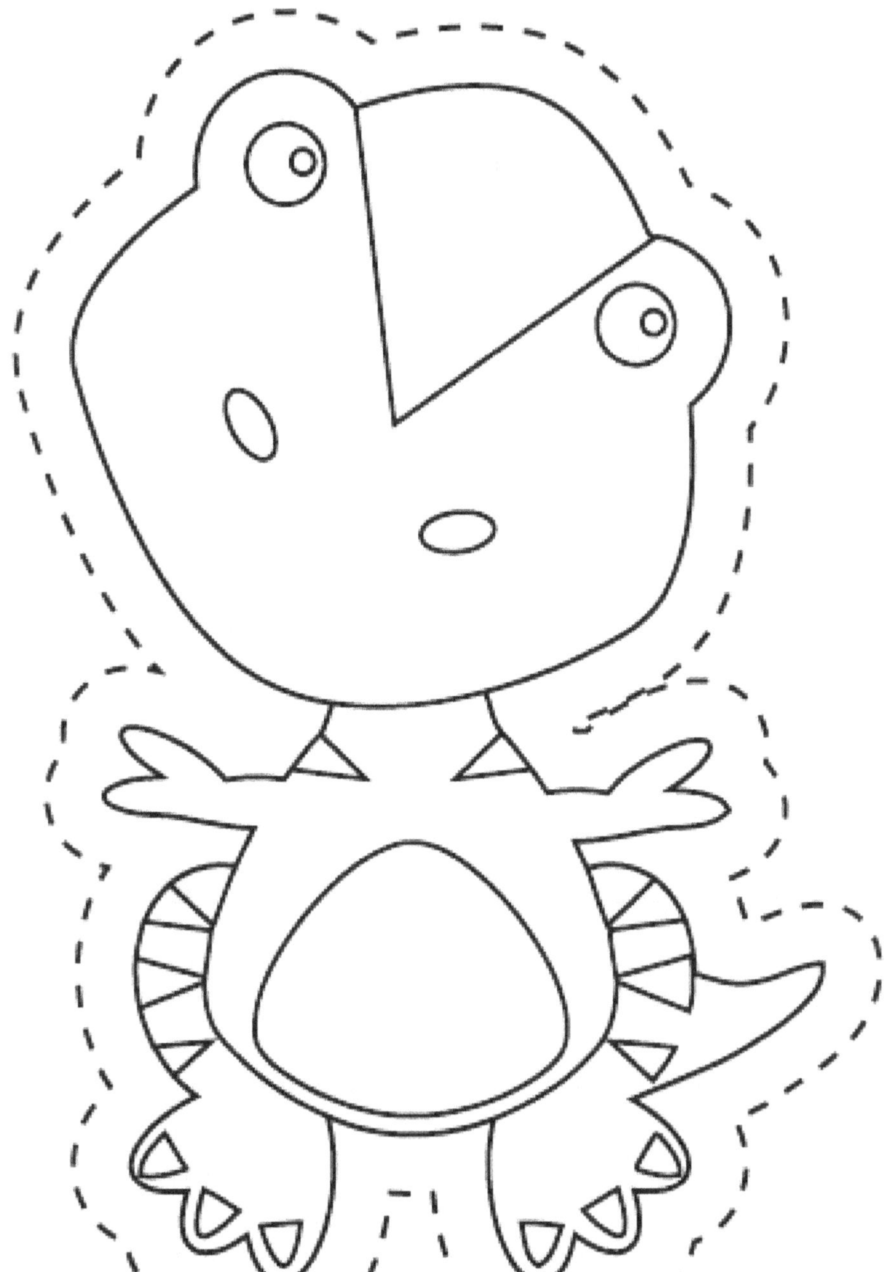

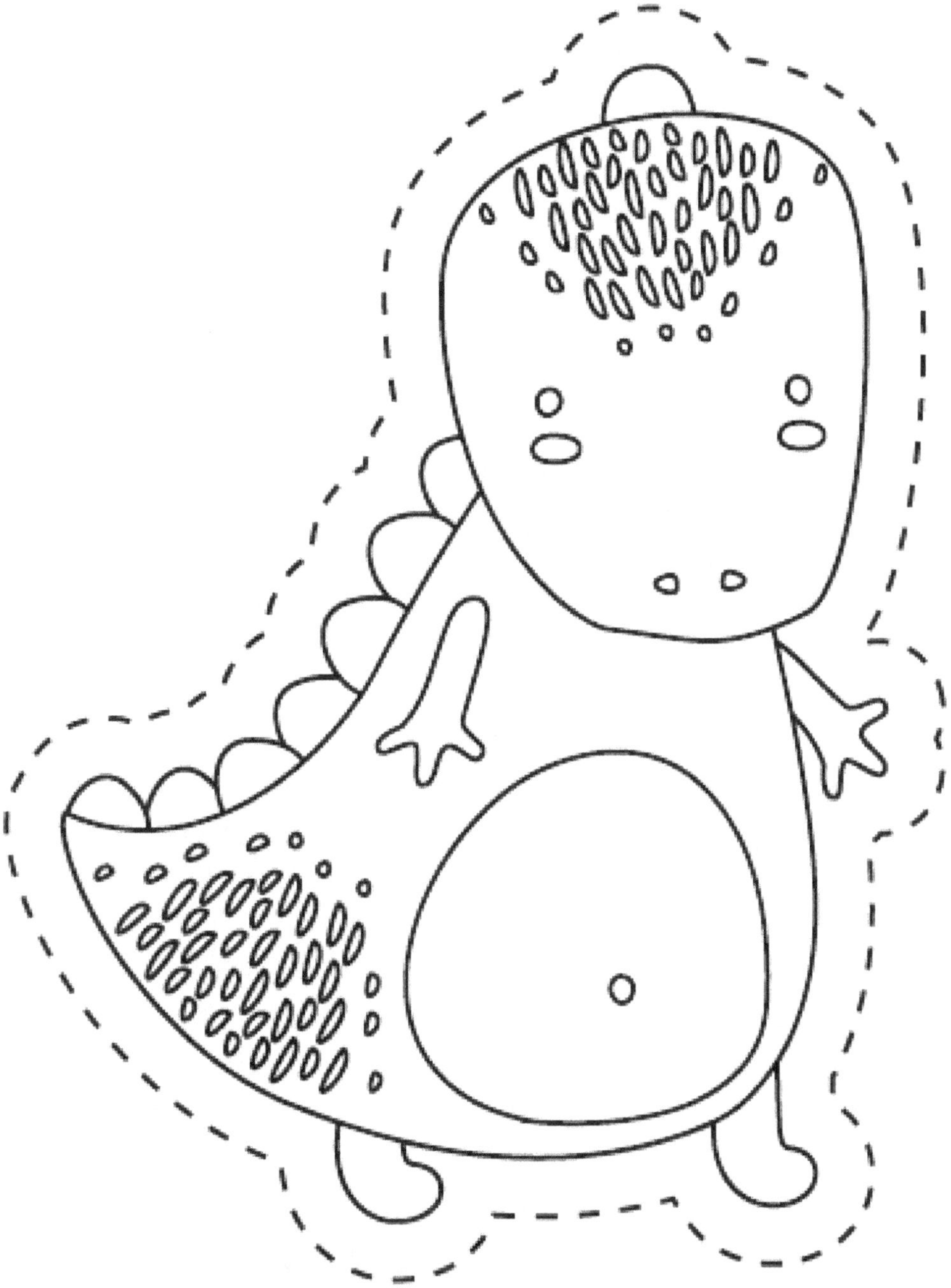

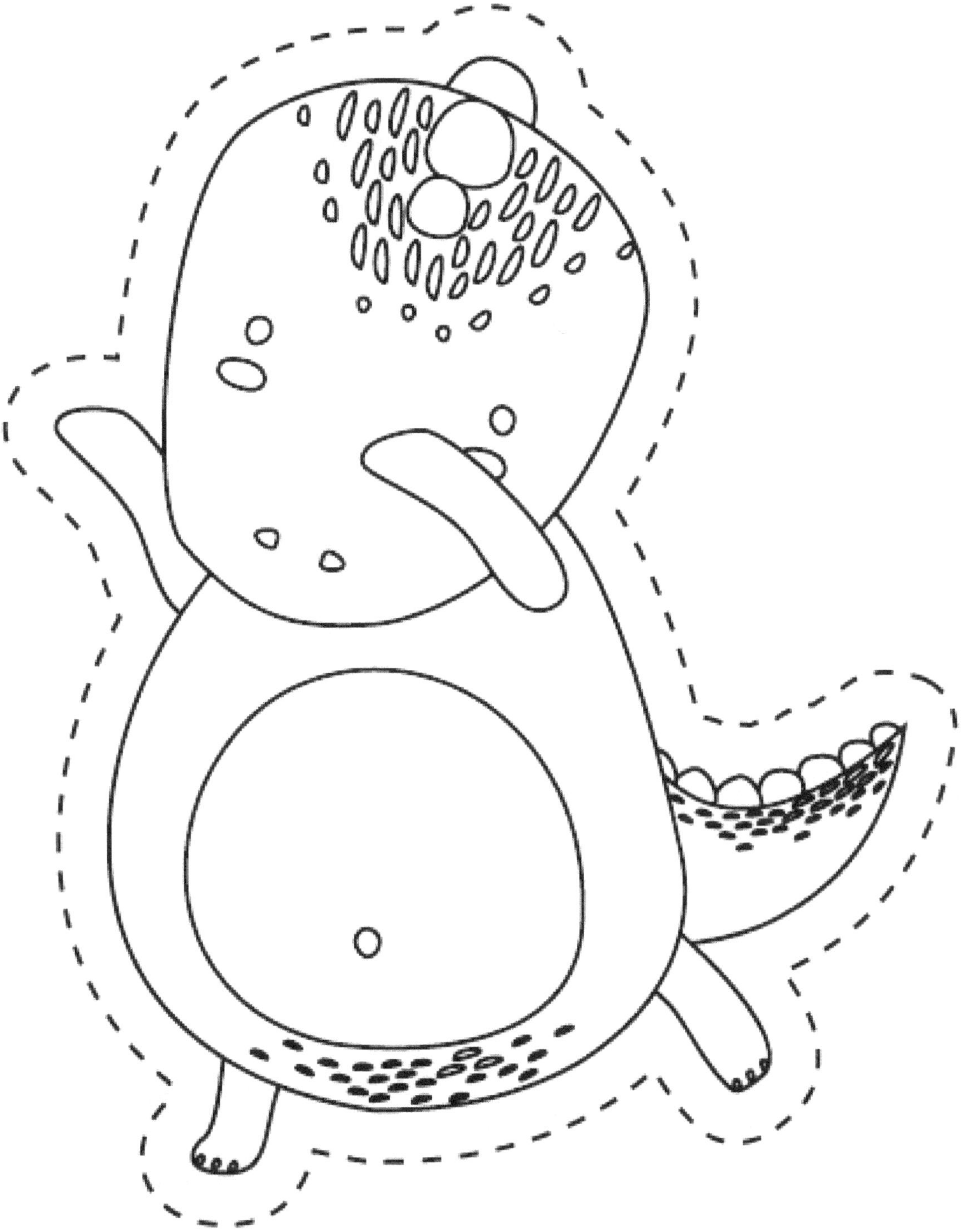

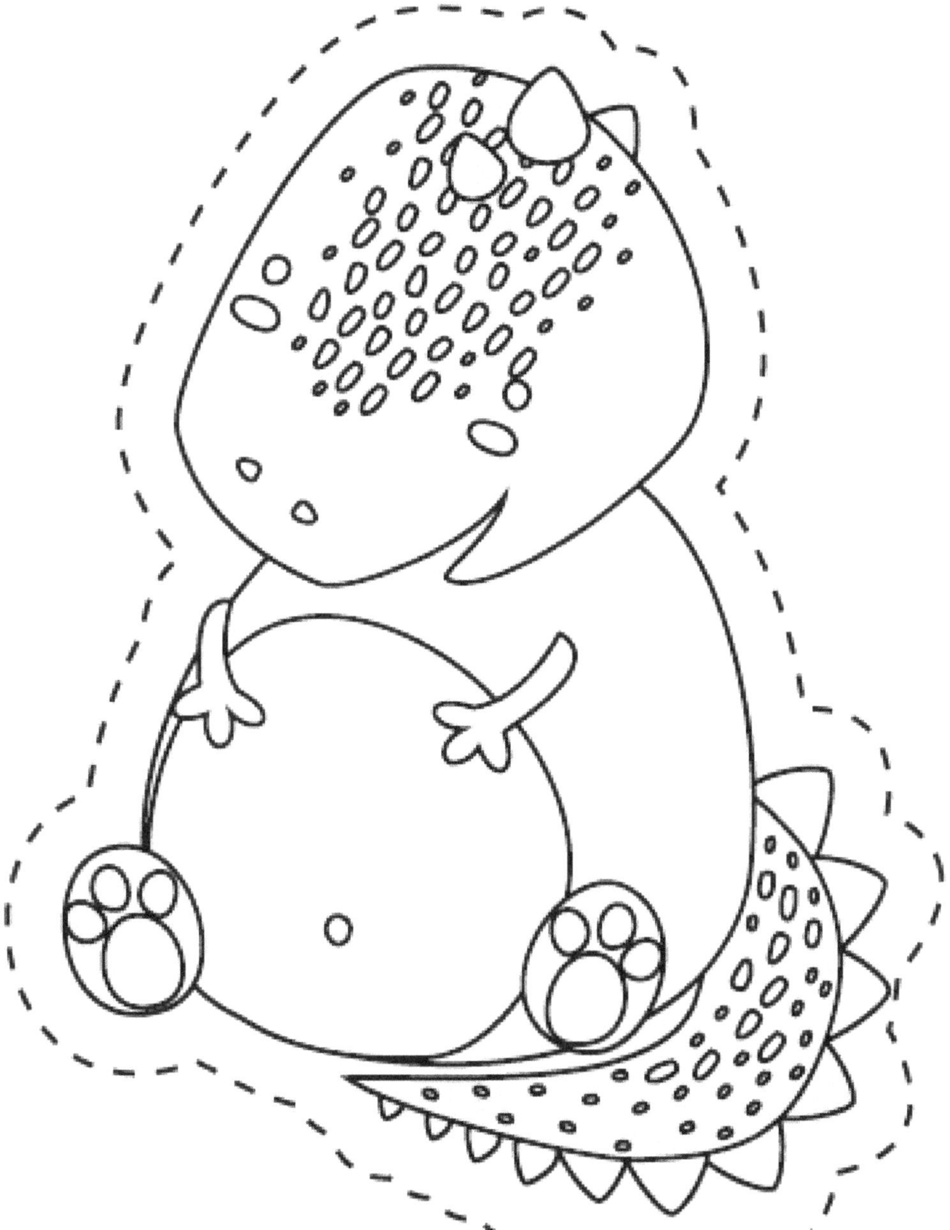

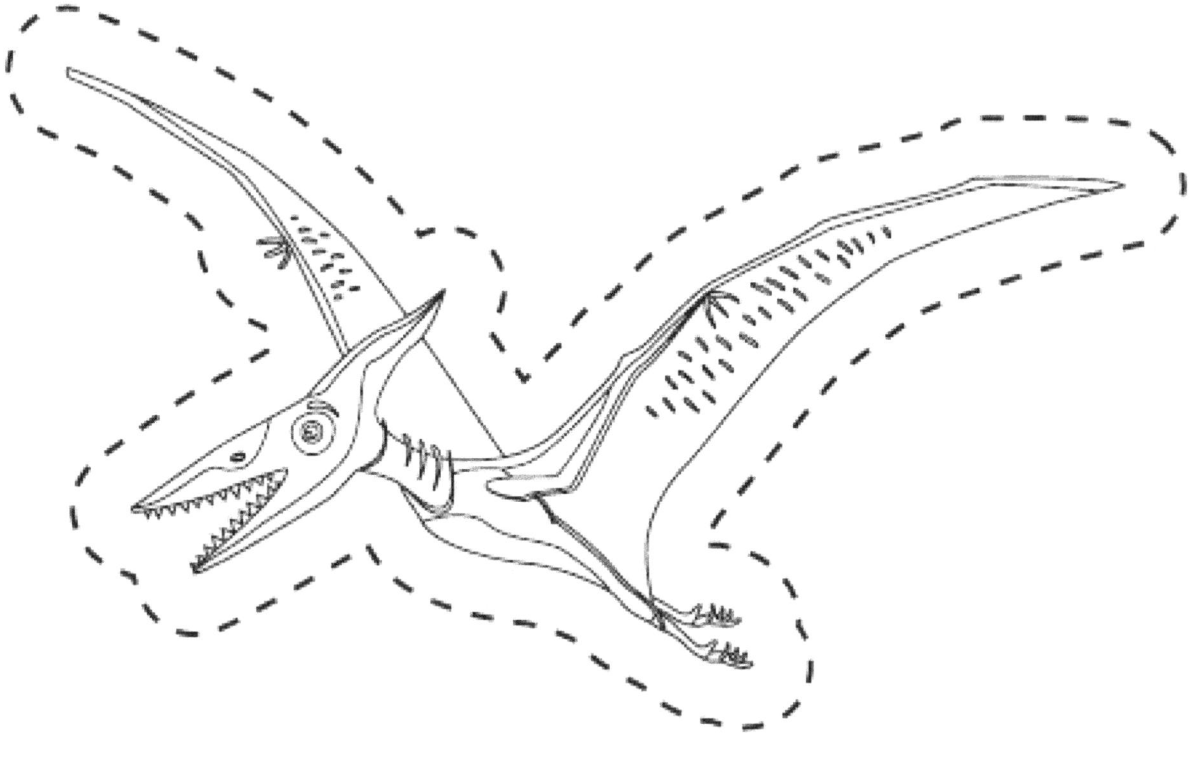

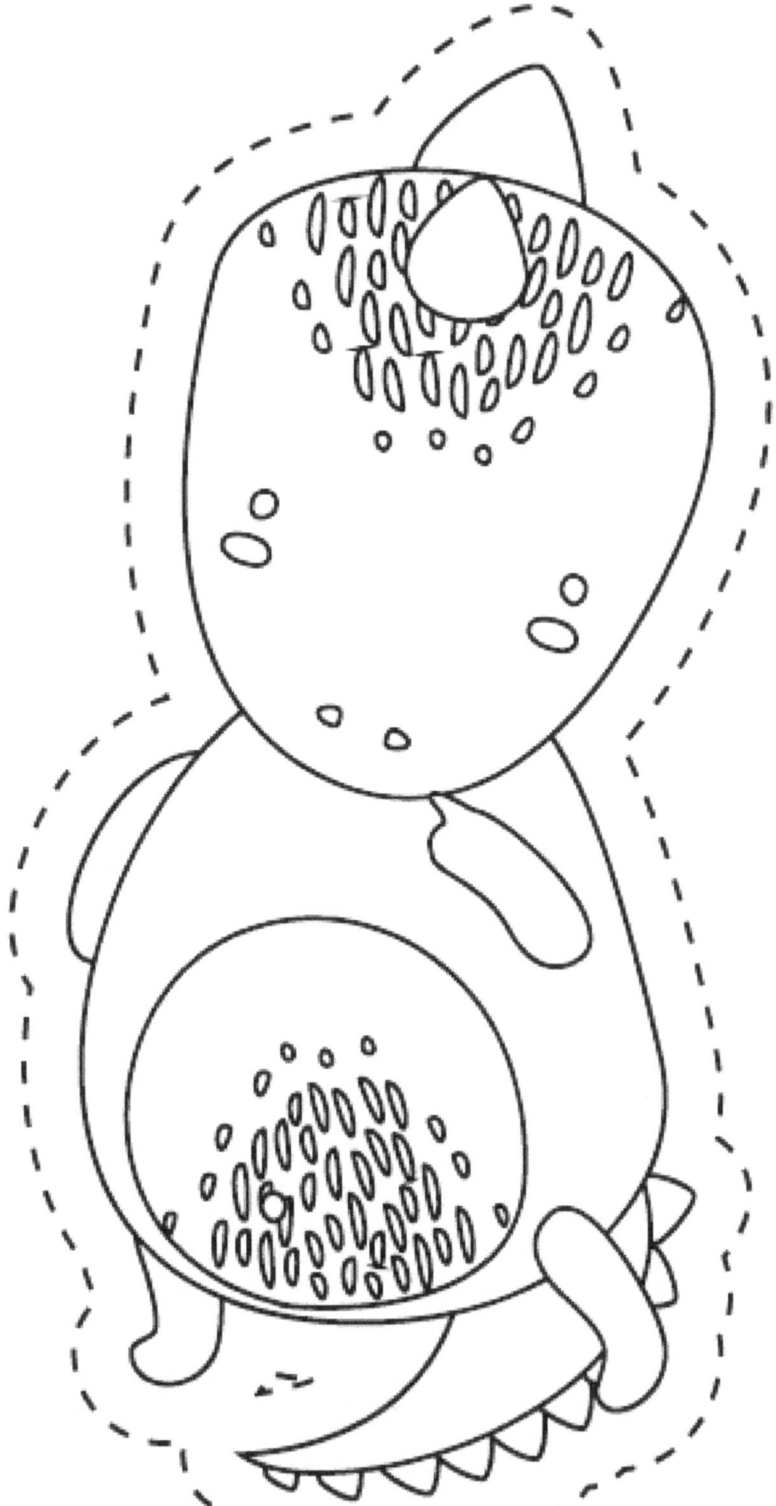

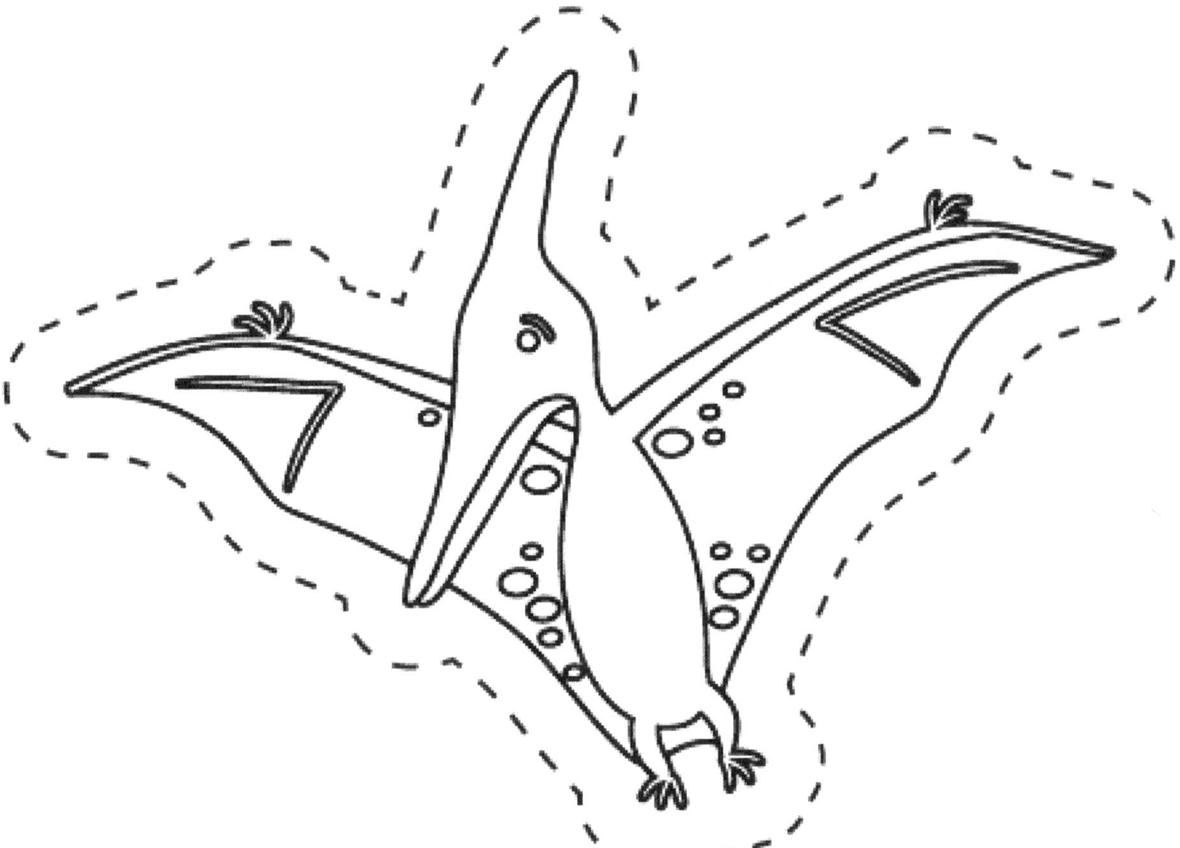

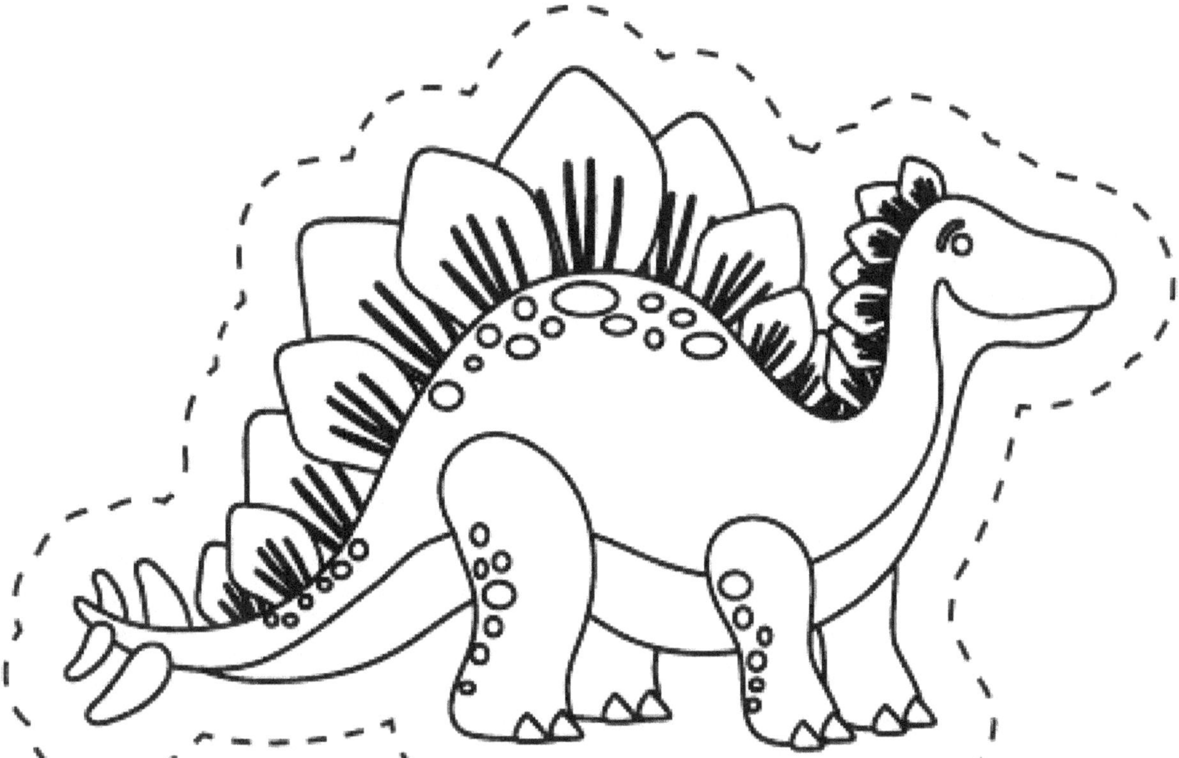

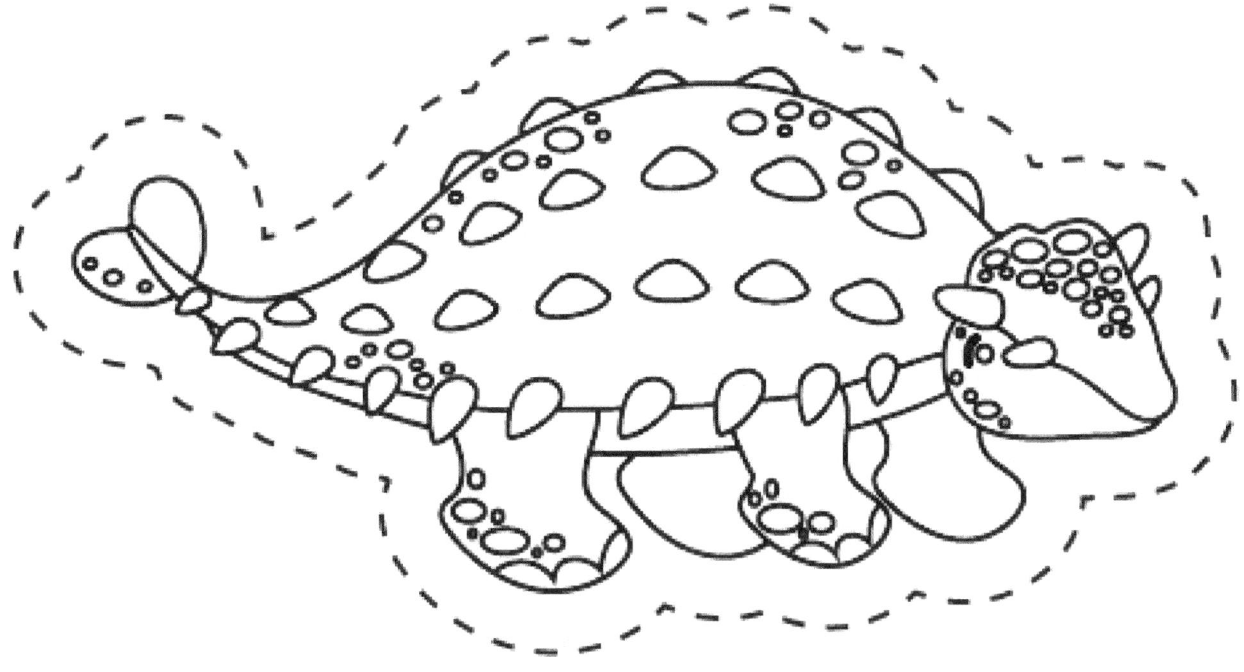

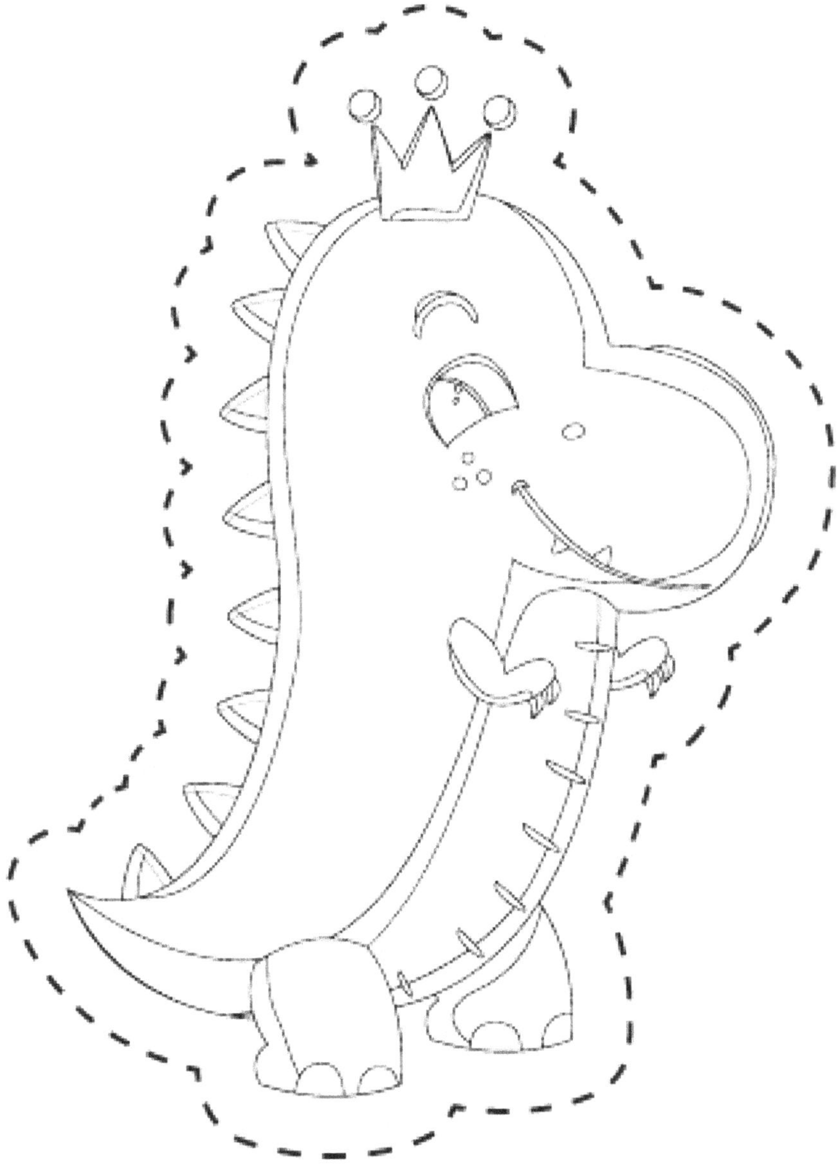

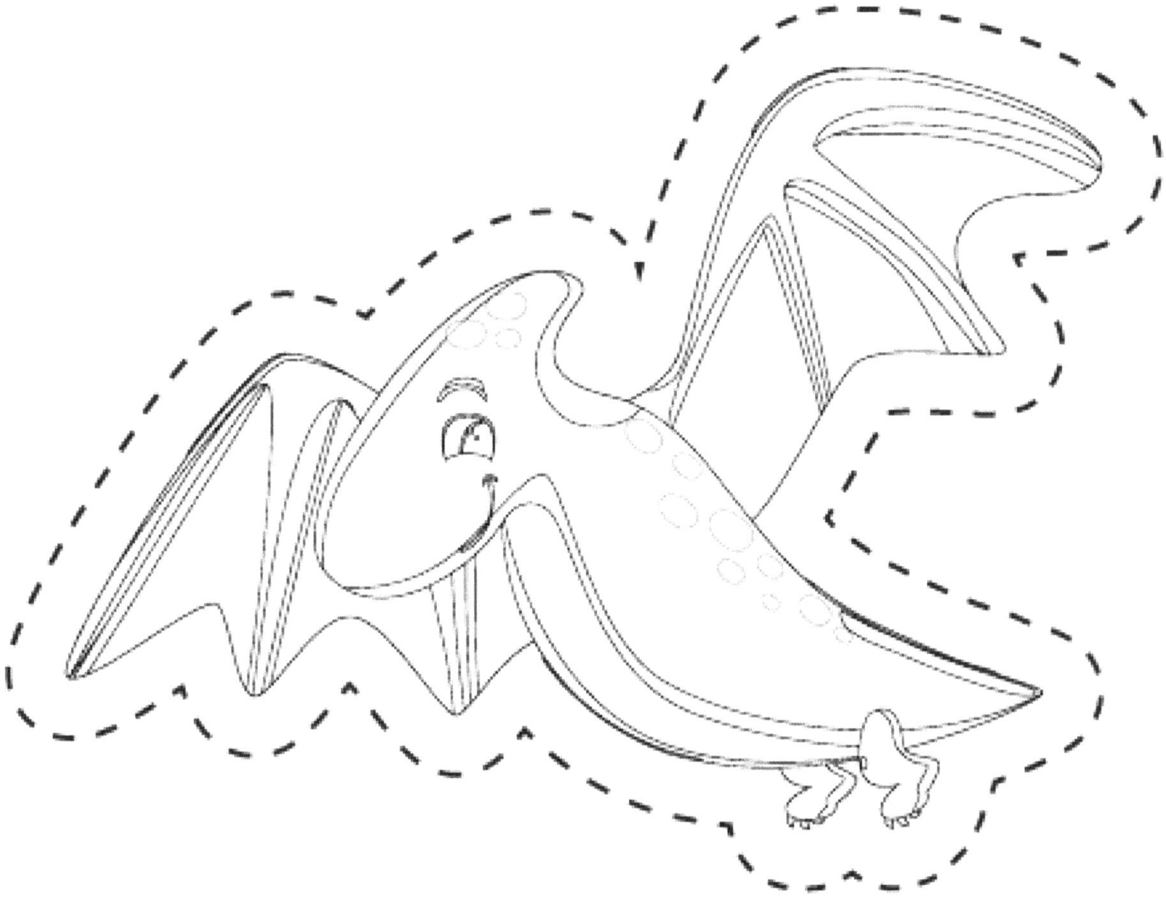

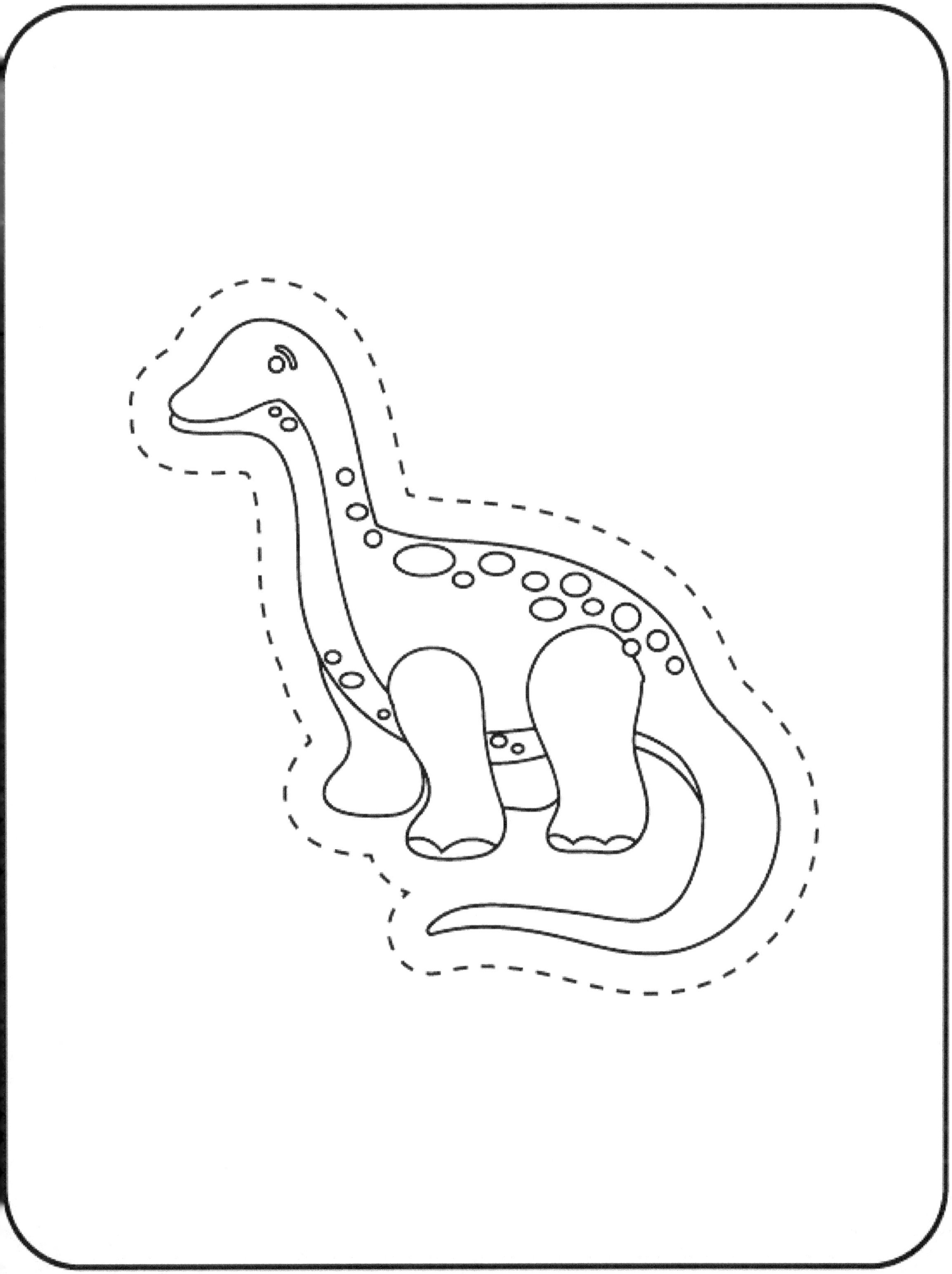

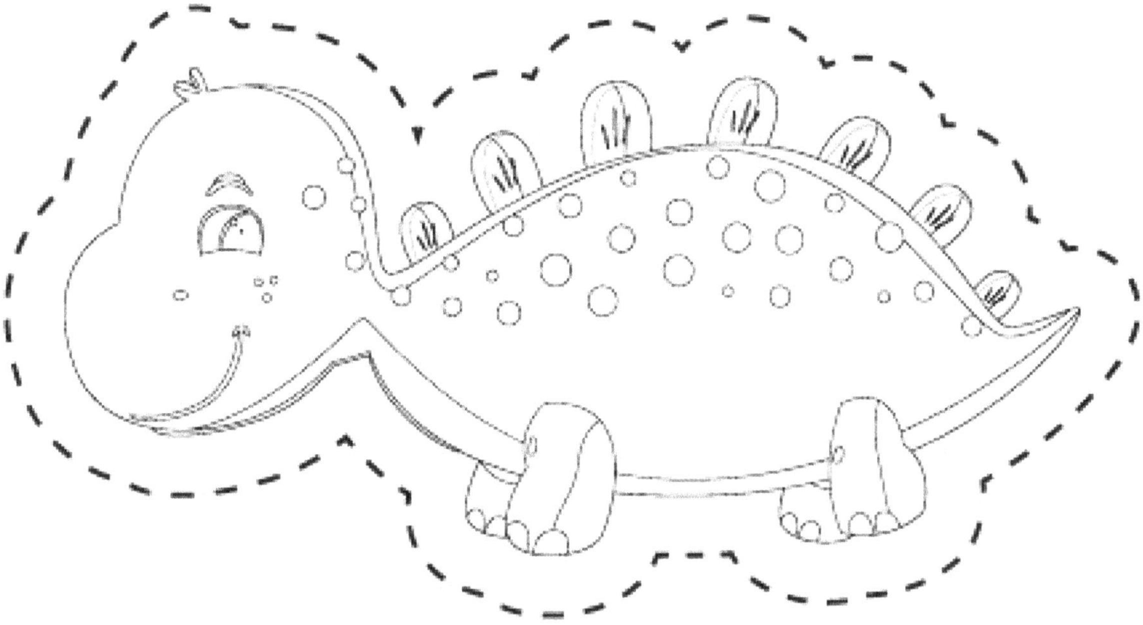

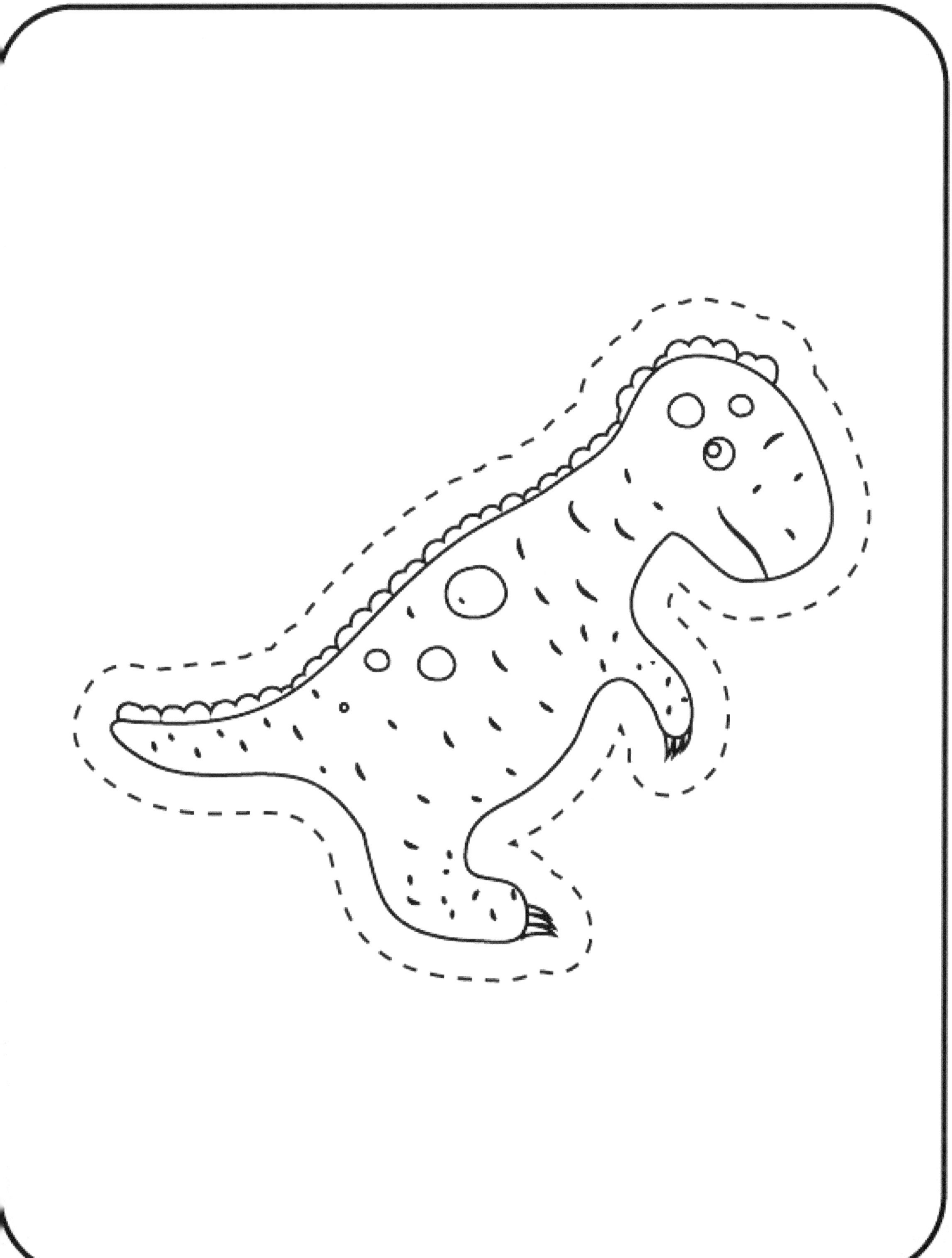

www.ingramcontent.com/pod-product-compliance
Lightning Source LLC
Chambersburg PA
CBHW080853220526
45467CB00008B/2498
* 9 7 9 8 7 1 4 7 7 8 4 0 7 *